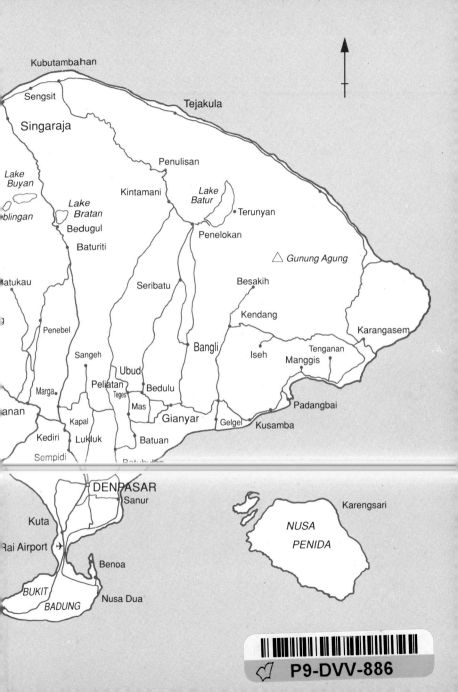

Flowers of Bali

Flowers of Bali

FRED AND MARGARET EISEMAN

PERIPLUS
EDITIONS
BERKELEY - SINGAPORE

Published by PERIPLUS EDITIONS
1442A Walnut Street #206
Berkeley, California 94709
The United States of America

Distributed in Indonesia by
JAVA BOOK DISTRIBUTORS
PO Box 55 JKCP
Jakarta 10510

PUBLISHER: Eric M. Oey
EDITED BY: Sylvia Tiwon
COVER: Pete Ivey
DESIGN: Pete Ivey and David Pickell
PRODUCTION: David Pickell
PHOTOGRAPHY: Fred and Margaret Eiseman

Library of Congress Catalog Card Number: 88-61080
ISBN: 0-945971-01-X

Printed in Singapore

Dedication

This book is dedicated to our friend and assistant, I Wayan Budiasa, Br. Teba, Jimbaran, Bali.

Over the years, Budi has become much more to us than a carrier of camera equipment, translator, driver, and generally indispensable helper. He has been our partner in every sense of the word. This book is typical of his work. Just about every flower we photographed was found by him; just about every piece of information about the flowers was translated by him; just about every still-life photograph was arranged by him. It is hard to imagine how much more important a person can be to anyone than Budi has been to us. And all the while, he went about his work with efficiency, humor, and tolerance of the odd ways of foreigners.

Budi has a knack for finding things and finding things out. We have but to ask him to take us to a place where there is a particularly interesting photographic subject, or where we can talk with someone who has some particularly important piece of information, and we are as good as there—even though Budi may never have been to the place nor known of the existence of the informant.

When we met Budi in the '70s, he was a taxi driver and we were not much more than tourists. We have come a long way together and dedicating this book to the person who was absolutely necessary in bringing it into existence is an appropriate way of saying:

Thanks, Budi. We appreciate everything you have done for us and for all those who read what you have helped us write and look at the pictures you have helped us take.

Table of Contents

Introduction

This is the second edition of *Flowers of Bali*. Extensive revisions have been made in the text and all photographs are new. Many flowers have been added, a few omitted, and the text and photographs have been arranged to facilitate flower identification.

There seems to be widespread satisfaction in the ability to name a flower. Conversely, the inability to put a label to an object is upsetting. However, there is a tendency to confuse the ability to name something with the ability to understand it. A name is only a symbol for a complex set of interlocking ideas or objects. Only if the symbol can be associated with these things is it useful. For this reason, the reader is encouraged to learn not just the names, but more about the flowers themselves—how they are used; why they are important; their origin and distribution.

No attempt has been made to make this book encyclopedic. There are descriptions and photographs of hundreds of flowers in our files. The purpose of this book is to help the foreign visitor identify the flowers he is most likely to see during his stay in Bali. We have traveled the by-ways of Bali for many years, and the inclusion or omission of a particular flower for this book is based only upon whether we think the average visitor is likely to see it. We have included a number of flowering trees of foreign origin because one sees them in bloom all along the major highways. We have omitted a number of flowers that are important and useful to the Balinese simply because they are either rare or inconspicuous, or because they are abundant only in areas not likely to be visited by the average tourist. We have also omitted most flowers which are already familiar to visitors because of their abundance in all parts of the world. There are lilies, begonias, zinnias, sunflowers, asters, roses, marigolds, and so on here, but these same flowers are common elsewhere, and thus, space is denied them in favor of flowers the visitor is not likely to have encountered previously. We would have liked to include the orchids. However, it is folly to speak about orchids as if they constitute a homogenous group. More than 3,000 species have been described, and it would have been impossible to speak about them in any but the most general terms.

Many visitors do not realize that tropical Bali has seasons. Bali is between eight and nine degrees south of the equator. During the months from approximately November through March, warm north-westerly winds sweep over the South China Sea and bring large amounts of rainfall to Bali. From about April to October, the Asian monsoon brings dry southeasterly winds up from the interior of the Australian subcontinent, and Bali then experiences a distinct dry period. Generally speaking, the best time to see most of the flowers in this book is during August and September, in the dry season. There are, of course, many exceptions.

Remember that plants are adapted to particular environments. You will only see some in the higher, cooler elevations. Others are only common to the sandy soils of the seashore. To see the majority of the flowers described here, you will have to visit places all throughout Bali. Our photographs were taken in widely scattered spots.

Most hotels have lovely gardens that are full of flowers. However, the emphasis in these gardens is on flowers that are long-lasting and relatively easy to care for. You are not likely to find large numbers of the flowers described in this book growing in and around tourist centers. You will find many of the flowering trees growing along the roadside because the Indonesian Department of Forestry has provided them for shade, forage, watershed protection, firewood, and beauty. You will find flowering plants and shrubs growing in house-compounds, school-yards, and in large fields where they are raised specifically for offerings. You may only see some of these flowers in the village market, as they grow on tall trees and are picked early in the morning.

Whatever your needs and your point of view, we hope the materials we have provided here are as interesting to you as they were to us

—*Fred and Margaret Eiseman*
1988

Acacia

The Balinese acacia is not native to the island but was introduced by the Indonesian Department of Forestry. It has adapted perfectly to its new environment. The By-Pass Highway is lined with vigorous specimens from Tohpati to Nusa Dua. It is a good shade tree and, like all legumes, helps to enrich the soil.

BALINESE: *akasia*
INDONESIAN: *pilang*
LATIN: *Acacia auriculiformis*
Family: *Leguminosae*

■**Description**: Distinctive yellow pendant clusters cover the medium-sized tree.

■**Flowers**: From a distance these look like long yellow pipe-cleaners or pieces of chenille. Each is actually a thin stem along which grow large numbers of tiny yellow flowers. The flower clusters are attached to twigs at leaf junctions and are about 1-2 cm apart. Each cluster is about 10 cm long and 8-9 cm in diameter. The individual flower is a few millimeters in size and has five petals curling from the flower cup. A fluff of yellow stamens protrudes from this cup.

■**Leaves**: Crescent-shaped, up to 18 by 3 cm. They are carried on short stems.

■**Seeds**: Contained in an unusually convoluted seed pod. As many as eight or 10 of these pods may be twisted around each other on the same stem.

■**Flowering**: In the middle of the dry season.

Adenium

Sometimes, mistakenly, frangipani

This is one of the three different trees the Balinese call *jepun*. The two others are *jepun bali* and *jepun jawa*. Although the adenium belongs to the same botanical family as the true frangipani, *Plumeria*, it is of an entirely different genus. In common with many members of the family *Apocynaceae*, the adenium (and the frangipani) exude a poisonous white latex when the branches are broken or damaged.

■**Description:** The general shape of this small tree is somewhat reminiscent of the frangipani, but unlike the *Plumeria*, the red or deep pink flowers have no odor.

■**Flowers:** Trumpet-shaped and generally of some shade of crimson, with edges somewhat darker than the center in some plants. One variety has pale pink flowers with streaks of white. The five petals are attached to a cup about 2.5 cm long and flare from 1 to 2 cm in diameter. The petals, which form an overlapping ring at the wide end, are almost dia-mond-shaped. The five sta-mens are fuzzy, long filaments that extend to the lip of the cup.

■**Leaves:** Club-shaped, about 12 by 4 cm, flaring out from a narrow base. The midrib is prominent. Leaves occur in bunches at the ends of rather fat branches.

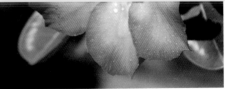

BALINESE: *jepun jepang*
INDONESIAN: not known
LATIN: *Adenium coetenium*; Family: *Apocynaceae*

African Tulip Tree

This native of tropical West Africa has been widely distributed along the roads of Bali by the Department of Forestry. It serves as a useful tall screen but requires good soil conditions for quick growth.

■**Description**: A free-flowering medium to tall tree with dense foliage and bearing orange-red flowers arranged in spikes at the ends of branches.

BALINESE: *kacret-kacretan*
INDONESIAN: *sepatu diat*
LATIN: *Spathodea campanulata*
Family: *Bignoniaceae*

■**Flowers**: Faintly fragrant, the flowers are reminiscent of tulips, forming large, orange-red cups about 7 cm long and 8 cm in diameter. The five petals are almost fused together. Inside the cup are four long stamens with dark-brown, T-shaped anthers and one long, thin, yellow pistil. The flower spike itself terminates in a cluster of brown buds, their tips extending outward and down to form a spherical mass that reminds one of a bear's claw. These buds contain a clear liquid that spurts out when the bud is broken. This is what gives the flower its Balinese name, which refers to the spurting of water.

■**Leaves**: Almost perfectly elliptical, about 5 by 10 cm, with a somewhat pointed end and prominent veins, carried on a thick stem.

■**Flowering**: August to October.

Allamanda

Also golden trumpet

The allamanda is a popular hotel plant and is frequently used in hedges. Although the flowers are beautiful, they are not often used in offerings. The entire plant is poisonous, but the vapor from its leaves is said to have cathartic value, good for curing coughs. It is a native of tropical America and its scientific name is derived from the Brazilian naturalist, Allamand, who popularized it in the early 1800s. He indicated that an infusion made from its leaves served as a good laxative. The plant can be found all over Bali.

■**Description**: A woody vine often winding through hedges or up trees. Depending on its support, it can reach 3 to 6 meters.

■**Flowers**: Bright yellow, bearing five rounded petals fused into a short funnel at their base. The entire flower is about 8 to 10 cm across. At the junction of the petals and the funnel there is often a large white spot and the petals are sometimes striped. Deep within the funnel is a fuzzy star bearing two hairy stamens and a green stigma on a long, white style. The flower has no noticeable fragrance.

■**Leaves**: Bright green and glossy on top, pale green underneath, usually pointed ovals up to 15 by 5 cm. They grow in clusters of four with very short stems.

BALINESE: *alamanda*
INDONESIAN: *alamanda*
LATIN: *Allamanda cathartica* L.; Family: *Apocynaceae*

Banana

There are dozens of varieties of bananas in Bali, most of which are far more flavorful than the rather bland plantation banana we are accustomed to in the West. The banana plant is not a tree, but rather, a giant herb. It produces fruit just once, then dies, leaving suckers at its base to start the next generation.

BALINESE: *biu*
INDONESIAN: *pisang*
LATIN: *Musa* sp.; Family: *Musaceae*

■**Description**: The deep red to maroon blooms appear about seven to nine months after planting. The flower stalk emerges from the crown of the plant, carrying the last leaves with it.
■**Flowers**: A large bud or "navel" develops at the tip of the stalk. As this *pusuh biu* (banana navel) develops, one of the outer bracts rises to reveal a double row of 12 to 29 female flowers with short-lasting, yellowish-white petals. This bract eventually drops. As the inflorescence grows, another bract folds upward, revealing another "hand" of female flowers. This continues until there are eight to 13 "hands." These are followed by several "hands" of neuter flowers, and then a long sequence of pollen-producing male flowers.
■**Leaves**: Young leaves are pale green and tightly rolled in cylindrical "buds" that unfurl into long, broad, dark green leaves.
■**Seeds**: The female flower of most bananas will produce fruit without pollination. Normally, one finds merely brown specks inside the fruits, but the hard black seeds of the variety *biu batu* present a hazard to the unwary eater.
■**Flowering**: Year-round.

Bougainvillea

This Brazilian native has spread all over the warmer parts of the world and can be seen everywhere in Bali. The flower's Balinese name, *kertas*, means "paper" and describes the texture of the colorful bracts. They are commonly used in offerings.

■**Description**: A highly ornamental shrub or vine that may grow up to several meters in height. Red is the most common variety but there are many plants with pink, peach or white flowers, or red and white may be mixed on the same plant. There is also a double variety in which the parts are multi-colored.

■**Flowers**: Each "flower" has three showy bracts with pointed ends, about 4.5 cm long and 2.5 cm wide. Each bract carries a single, inconspicuous flower at its base. The actual flower is tubular, 3 cm long and about 3 mm wide, ending in a flared portion consisting of 5 lobes and 5 shorter petals with wrinkled edges situated between the lobes. The entire flower is white, except for the 5 larger lobes which are striped on the outside. Just visible inside the tube are five thin stamens and one pistil.

■**Leaves**: are oval, about 4 cm long and 2.3 cm wide, dark green. Veining is not prominent. Leaves are borne singly on 1.5 cm stems.

BALINESE: *kertas*
INDONESIAN: *buganvil*
LATIN: *Bougainvillea spectabilis*; Family: *Nyctaginaceae*

Calliandra

The Indonesian Department of Forestry has introduced two species of calliandra to the island. Being legumes, they help to fertilize the soil and their flowers attract bees. Calliandra is native to tropical America.

BALINESE: *kaliandra*
INDONESIAN: not known
LATIN: *Calliandra* sp.; Family: *Leguminosae*

■**Description**: Two varieties of calliandra are fairly common in Bali. The powder puff calliandra, *Calliandra surinamensis*, is a woody shrub that grows up to about 2 meters in height. *C. calothyrsa* (pictured here) is more common than the powder puff and is more like a tree. Its flowers grow in a spike up to 12 cm long.

■**Flowers**: The distinctive flowers of the powder puff are tufts colored magenta on top and white at the base. Each tuft contains what appear to be large numbers of thin hairs, about 3 cm long. Close examination reveals that these are actually 30 separate flowers, each with a white, 3 cm-long tube bearing a serrated cup at its end. From this cup protrude 13 red stamens, each about 1.5 cm long. *C. calothyrsa* flowers are borne on very short stems branching out from the main stalk in clumps of six. Each stalk bears 3-7 flowers. The individual flower consists of a tiny yellow-green cup from which protrudes a mass of bright red stamens tipped with bright yellow anthers.

■**Leaves**: Doubly compound with narrow oval leaflets, 4 mm by 13 mm.

■**Seeds**: Contained in flat, club-shaped pods, about 9 cm by 1 cm.

Canna

The canna is a native of South America and is now wide-spread throughout Southeast Asia. In some areas it is raised commercially for its rhizomes, which can be cooked and eaten or rendered into a starchy flour. The seeds are sometimes drilled and strung to form a set of prayer beads, a use which has inspired the Indonesian name—*bunga tasbih*—which comes from an Arabic term for "prayer beads."

■**Description**: This is a perennial herb with considerable variation in the size and shape of its flower parts.

■**Flowers**: Red, white, or yellow and, in general, about 10 cm in diameter and about 12 cm long, with three or four large, oval petals which may be striped at the edges or in the center. Surrounding these are three much smaller petals, rolled into pointed cones. Covering the base of the flower is a papery green sheath that envelops a barrel-shaped ovary. This ovary is about 1.5 cm long and 1 cm in diameter. Its surface is covered with tiny knobs.

■**Leaves**: Long and green. There is also a variety with maroon leaves and stems.

■**Seeds**: Contained in the hardened globular ovary. These are difficult to sprout and the plant is generally propagated by rhizome.

BALINESE: *soga*

INDONESIAN: *bunga tasbih, kana*

LATIN: *Canna orientalis*; Family: *Cannaceae*

Cassia

This tree is one of the three members of the large genus *Cassia* which are common to Bali. It was imported by the forestry department and planted along many of the roads. Throughout Asia it is used as a shade tree because it grows easily and rapidly, attaining a height of three meters in just two years.

BALINESE: *kasia*
INDONESIAN: not known
LATIN: *Cassia siamea*; Family: *Leguminosae*

■**Description**: A medium-sized tree that produces conical spikes of yellow blossoms at the ends of its branches.
■**Flowers**: Each is about 4 to 4.5 cm in diameter and has 5 bright yellow petals shaped like tear-drops. Usually, although there is some variation, there are six or seven short, thick, white stamens with large brown anthers. The pistil is pale green and longer than the stamens. Below the petals are five small, green sepals, triangular in shape with rounded ends.
■**Leaves**: Consist of small, oval leaflets about 4 by 2 cm, growing in pairs along the main stem. They are medium green.
■**Seeds**: are borne in pods about 15-20 cm long and 2 cm wide.
■**Flowering**: Towards the end of the dry season, starting in September and reaching its peak in October.

Champak

In Bali, this tree is chiefly used as a source of fragrant flowers. In fact, one has to learn to recognize the tree by its shape and leaves because it is usually denuded of flowers. Its flowers are among the most fragrant of all those in Bali and are popular in offerings. They are sold in all markets. In performances, the beard of the *barong* is often decorated with these flowers. A volatile oil is extracted from the flowers for use in perfumes and hair oil. The bark has medicinal properties and is used to prepare an anti-fever drink.

■**Description**: The tree is 15 to 25 m high and thus the flowers are not easily seen from the ground. There are two varieties of champak: pure white and golden yellow. Moreover, there are two varieties of white champak, one having smaller flowers.

■**Flowers**: The buds are completely enclosed within a tight-fitting sheath that bursts open when the flower blooms. The sheath is some-what ribbed with a faint where the split will occur.

BALINESE: *capaka*
INDONESIAN: *cempaka*
LATIN: *Michelia champaca* L.; Family: *Magnoliaceae*

Generally, there are several concentric circles of petals, each successive circle being smaller than the previous one. The most common arrangement is four or five large petals on the outside, four or five slightly smaller ones within, and several tiny petals in the third circle. The larger white or yellow flowers are up to 11 cm in diameter. The smaller ones are only 3.5 cm long and 1 cm in diameter before they open.

■**Leaves**: Light green, oval, about 10 cm wide and 22 cm long, pointed at both ends and attached to the twig by a 2 cm stem.

■**Flowering**: Year-round.

Chenille Plant

Also monkey's tail, or cat's tail

This plant, which originated in the West Indies, has become common in Bali. It can be seen in house yards and gardens, where it is grown as an ornamental.

BALINESE: *ikut lutung*
INDONESIAN: *ekor kera*
LATIN: *Acalypha hispida*
Family: *Euphorbiaceae*

■**Description**: This medium shrub produces numerous tassels that droop down like tails from the plant.

■**Flowers**: each tassel consists of many small red flowers distributed closely along a stem up to 50 cm long and 1 cm in diameter. The "tails" look like bright red pipe cleaners because of the unbelievably large number of thin red hairs that are attached to the flowers. The individual flower is a fuzzy white sphere only about 2 mm in diameter with four hairy sepals underneath. Three branches of red filaments project from the top of this white ball. The total length of ball and filament is about 5 mm. There are about 800 of these tiny balls on each flowering raceme. Once the flowers mature and go to seed, the "monkey tails" look a little shaggy and worn.

■**Leaves**: Serrated, spear-shaped and red-veined, occuring alternately on 6 cm stems. The largest are 20 cm long and 16 cm wide.

Climbing Lily

Also gloriosa lily

The vine grows from a white bulb which contains the poisonous chemical, colchicine, a gastro-intestinal irritant. The leaves are, reportedly, used as a traditional medicine to kill head-lice. The Balinese and Indonesian names for this flower mean "upside down," and apt description because the petals grow upward while the stamens and pistil point down.

■**Description**: A medium shrub or climbing vine.

■**Flowers**: The red, orange, or yellow flowers have six crinkled petals, about 6.5 cm long and 1.2 cm wide. When the flower first opens, the petals are green; as it matures, they turn yellow with red tips. Older flowers are a uniform red. Six stamens, about 4 cm long, end in a T-shaped anther. The pistil is green with a 5 cm long style and a three-lobed stigma.

■**Leaves**: Medium green and thin, reaching a length of 25 cm. The tips of the leaves are prehensile, and wraps themselves around objects to provide support for the vine.

■**Seeds**: Yellowish-red and contained in pods which look like long, green chili peppers.

■**Flowering**: During the rainy season in the wild. With regular watering, these plants may bloom all year.

BALINESE: *sungsang, sungsiang*
INDONESIAN: *kembang sungsang, kembang jonggrang*
LATIN: *Gloriosa superba*; Family: *Liliaceae*

Cock's Comb

The cock's comb is grown as an ornamental and used principally in gardens, although some may be found growing wild along the roads. The Balinese name—*janggar siap*—like the English, describes the flower's appearance, which in some varieties forms a wavy crest.

BALINESE: *janggar siap*
INDONESIAN: *jengger ayam*
LATIN: *Celosia argentea*; Family: *Amarantaceae*

■**Description**: A small ornamental.

■**Flowers**: The flowering part of the plant is a giant brush with small, bright red or crimson bristles. There are two varieties: one has a rather simple flowering top that forms finger-like projections. The other is fan-shaped, often quite wavy. Both varieties are quite low, growing to a height of between 40-140 cm. There are red, yellow and lavender varieties. The flowering head consists of large masses of tiny flowers, each only about 2 mm in diameter. The uppermost flowers are unopened, so that all one sees is the bright color of the outside of their petals. Still farther down is the magenta pistil.

■**Leaves**: Spear-shaped and slightly wrinkled, up to 16 by 6 cm.

■**Seeds**: Each ovary contains five tiny seeds which can be shaken from the flower.

■ **Flowering**: Year-round.

Coconut

The mature coconut is used in cooking and the young fruit as a refreshing drink. The still immature leaves, not yet separated into the distinctive fronds, are used in preparing offerings and ceremonial decorations. The tiny offering baskets seen all over Bali are cut from coconut leaves and pinned together with bits of bamboo.

■**Description**: The inflorescence of this tree begins from the base of the older leaves, and before opening, looks like a gigantic corn cob, its surface ridged lengthwise and tapering to a sharp point. The Balinese call this *danggul*, which, depending on the variety, is from 50 to 75 cm long and about 7 to 8 cm in diameter. The sheath, called *keloping* in Balinese, is flexible before opening. It gradually hardens and eventually splits.

■**Flowers**: A split *keloping* reveals a densely packed mass of about 40 white to yellowish-tan stalks, each about 40 cm long, attached to a central, thicker stem. The upper two-thirds of each of these stalks is completely covered with small male flowers, each enclosed in three tiny triangular bracts. One stalk has about 250 of these

BALINESE: *nyuh*
INDONESIAN: *kelapa, nyiur*
LATIN: *Cocos nucifera*; Family: *Palmae*

flowers. These male flowers begin to mature and open immediately, starting at the top. As the bracts open, six short, curled yellow stamens are revealed. Each has an enlarged anther bearing pollen. Young trees that flower for the first time produce only male flowers. After a few years, one or two smooth knobs may be seen at the base of the stalk which are the female flowers. After fertilization, sheaths, called *tapuk nyuh* in Balinese, develop around most of the knob, leaving only a small, triangular area exposed at the tip. This tip exudes nectar.

■**Leaves**: Long, dark green fronds, very pale yellowish-green when immature.

■**Seeds**: The familiar coconut covered by a husk which starts out green and gradually darkens to a somewhat orange/green color, becoming bright orange in some varieties. It takes one year for a coconut to reach maturity.

Coffee

Most of the world's coffee comes from one of the two species of the genus *Coffea*. Westerners are likely to be most familiar with *Coffea arabica* because this is the type that is widely imported from Brazil and Colombia. *C. robusta* is less familiar and is popularly called *kopi bali*. The largest *robusta* planting area is in the Pupuan area; the center of *arabica* production in Bali is just north of Kintamani.

BALINESE: *kopi*
INDONESIAN: *kopi*
LATIN: *Coffea* sp.; Family: *Rubiaceae*

■**Description**: Wild varieties of coffee grow up to 3 or 4 m high, while the cultivated types are trimmed to about half this height, which increases production and facilitates picking the beans.
■**Flowers**: Appear at leaf-pair junctions, clinging tightly to the twigs. They are pure white and quite fragrant, with no hint in their scent of the coffee brew. The flowers occur in dense clusters, 6 or 7 cm in diameter. Each individual flower has five thin, white petals forming a star about 3 cm in diameter. This star is attached to a thin, white, pentagonal tube, about 1 cm long. Five thin stamens with dark, T-shaped anthers protrude above the top of this tube. There is a single white pistil with a double tip.
■**Leaves**: *Robusta* (the most common variety in Bali) leaves are about 20 cm long and 9 cm wide, oval, tapering to a sharp, pointed tip. They are medium to dark green and glossy. *Arabica* has similar but smaller leaves, about 13 by 6 cm.
■**Seeds**: Contained in a sweet, juicy berry tasting not at all of coffee.
■**Flowering**: April to September or October.

Coral Hibiscus

This plant is of the same species as the more common *Hibiscus rosa-sinensis*, the common flowering hibiscus. The coral hibiscus gets its Balinese name from a combination of *pucuk*, the Balinese name for the familiar hibiscus, and *geringsing*, a double tie-dyed fabric woven in the village of Tenganan. The Balinese associate this flower with magic and the practitioners of "black magic" are said to use it.

■**Description**: The plant resembles the common hibiscus and is either a shrub or vine, growing to several meters in height.

■**Flowers**: These are red, about 7 cm in diameter, and dangle face down from long, thin stalks. The flowers are not cup-shaped like the common hibiscus but have five lacy petals which curve out and around the edge of the flower blossom. Each petal is deeply cut in long, narrow lobes. The pistil is 8 cm long, has a complex stigma of five segments and protrudes straight down from the drooping blossom. The stamens grow, bristle-like, around its tip.

■**Leaves**: Serrated half-way toward the tip, medium to dark green, about 5.5 by 2.5 cm, although leaves on new wood tend to be larger.

■**Flowering**: Year-round.

BALINESE: *pucuk geringsing*
INDONESIAN: *kembang lampu*
LATIN: *Hibiscus schizopetalus*; Family: *Malvaceae*

Coral Tree

The most important of the four species of coral tree common to Bali is the one the Balinese call *dadap kayu sakti*. This tree, *Erythrina subumbrans*, is a symbol of life-energy, perhaps because of its vitality—a bare stick thrust into the ground quickly takes root, sprouts leaves and grows into a full-sized tree. The leaf-bearing branches in particular are used in a variety of Balinese ceremonies. The chopped leaves and the flowers are used in offerings and in medicines.

BALINESE: *dadap, dapdap*
INDONESIAN: *dadap, dedap*
LATIN: *Erythrina* sp.; Family: *Leguminosae*

■**Description**: A medium-tall, thorny tree.
■**Flowers**: In the center of the red flowering part is a star that has about nine radial branches. When mature, each branch terminates in a red tip from which a petal grows. The petal is bright red, about 3 cm long. It curls under along the edges, forming a cavity which contains about 10 white stamens and one pistil. Several of these structures will often be visible on one stalk.
■**Leaves:** Almost round, with a point at the end, about 12 by 8 cm.
■**Seeds**: Contained in short, bean-like pods.
■**Flowering:** In villages, the foliage is in such demand for ceremonies that the flowers are never given a chance to develop. The flowers can be seen only in remote areas.

Datura

Also angel's trumpet

The datura belongs to the same family as the deadly night-shade. These plants contain the poisonous alkaloid scopolamine. Used in controlled amounts, this chemical produces powerful hallucinations. Because of this property, the drug has had religious connections in various parts of the world. However, if it is misused or accidentally eaten, it can cause death.

■**Description**: A tall, woody shrub that can reach a height of several meters.

■**Flowers**: Nodding trumpets up to 25 cm long flaring out to a diameter of about 13 cm with five sharp points. The Balinese name, *kecubung*, refers to the funnel-shaped acoustic loudspeakers of the early phonograph days—this perfectly describes the flower's shape. They may be all white or white with pink-ish-peach parts. One variety is entirely pink. The outer base of the flower is covered with a large green sheath ending in five triangular tips. Within the flower are five slender stamens, about 20 cm long, bearing brown, woolly anthers. The white pistil extends 1.5 cm beyond the stamens.

■**Leaves**: Spear-shaped with a pointed tip, about 24 cm long and 12 cm wide.

BALINESE: *kecubung, semprong*
INDONESIAN: *kecubung*
LATIN: *Datura suaveolens*; Family: *Solanaceae*

Datura

This datura, called *kecubung bali* by the Balinese, is very poisonous, as it contains an even greater concentration of the potentially lethal alkaloid, scopolamine, than its relative, *Datura suaveolens*. Because of the ability of the drug to induce hallucinations, datura is associated with religious experiences.

■**Description**: This plant is very similar to its close relative, *Datura suaveolens*, but it is smaller, reaching a height of no more than one meter.
■**Flowers**: Off-white, 10 cm long, conical trumpets, about 5 cm across at the flare. Its base is covered by a 5 cm, green sheath. Inside the flower are 5 white stamens with tan anthers and one white, 6 cm pistil with a green stigma.
■**Leaves**: Medium green, spear-shaped, about 18 cm long and 14 cm wide, with prominent veins. They are borne on 7 cm long stems.
■**Seeds**: Carried in a spherical fruit up to 4.5 cm in diameter and studded with protrusions. When the dried fruit splits, small tan seeds are released.

BALINESE: *kecubung bali, kecubung cenik*
INDONESIAN: not known
LATIN: *Datura metel*; Family: *Solanaceae*

Firecracker Hibiscus

This plant is often grown as a hedge. The flower produces a sweet nectar which children like to taste. The crushed leaves produce a liquid that looks like coconut oil. The Balinese name, *pucuk tabia-tabia*, means "chili pepper" which refers to the shape and color of the blossoms.

■**Description**: A shrub bearing flowers that look like the unopened flowers of the common red hibiscus.

■**Flowers**: Cylindrical, with the pistil protruding like the fuse of a firecracker. The petals form a tight left-handed spiral about 7 cm long and 1.5 cm across. Each petal is more or less triangular in shape and is about 5 cm long and 2.4 cm wide at the tip. At the base of the flower are two sets of saw-toothed concentric sepals, five to eight on the outside and five within. The outermost sepals are long triangles. The pistil is about 6 cm long, its stigma divided into five black tips. A cluster of short stamens with black anthers is found below the tip of the pistil.

BALINESE: *pucuk tabia-tabia*
INDONESIAN: *kembang lampu*
LATIN: *Malvafiscus* sp.; Family: *Malvaceae*

■**Leaves**: Tear-drop shaped with a rounded base, serrated, 9 to 12 cm long and 4 to 8 cm wide. They are medium green with prominent veining underneath.

■**Flowering**: Year-round.

Flamboyant

Also royal poinciana, or flame tree

The flamboyant is a native of Madagascar but was distrubuted all over the tropics during the 19th century. The tree's wide-spreading branches make it ideal for shade. They are planted along many of the main roads and, where they do well, the branches form an almost closed arch.

BALINESE: *flamboyan, merak*
INDONESIAN: *flamboyan, merak*
LATIN: *Delonix regia*; Family: *Leguminosae*

■**Description:** A medium tree with spreading branches and a rounded crown.
■**Flowers**: Red, 7-8 cm in diameter, with five petals. Four petals are identical and spaced symmetrically. Each consists of a long, thin strip ending in a wavy-edged oval and is a uniform red. A fifth petal is streaked with white near the edges and is yellow near the narrow strip. Below the petals are five sepals, about 2.2 cm long, red on top and green at the bottom. Ten stamens, about 4 cm long and red, protrude from the flower and terminate in mushroom-shaped, blackish anthers. The pistil is pink, about 5 cm long, and ends in a green stigma.
■**Leaves**: Compound, consisting of small, oval leaflets occuring in pairs along the stems. They are pale green when young, darken as they mature, and eventually turn bright yellow.
■**Seeds**: Contained in long, dark-brown pods.
■**Flowering**: Late in the dry season, beginning about the middle of September. Flowers are most profuse in November.

Four O'clock

This native American herb is now found everywhere in the tropics. It grows from large tubers. Both the Indonesian and English names refer to the fact that the flower opens in the late afternoon. However, it is not unusual to find some flowers opening early in the morning, whence, another common name in Indonesian, *pagi sore*—"morning, afternoon." The Latin name of the plant is a result of confusion between its large tubers and those of jalap, a Mexican vine that was brought into Europe to be used as a laxative. The four o'clock is strictly ornamental.

■**Description**: This plant seldom grows more than 50 cm high.

■**Flowers**: Deep rose-red, trumpet-shaped, about 5 cm long and 2 cm across. The five petals are almost completely fused together into a tube. Inside the flower are five fine stamens, each about 3 cm long. These are difficult to see becasue they are coiled within the flower. The pistil is about 4.5 cm long.

■**Leaves**: Spear-shaped, 7 cm long and 3 cm wide, with sharply pointed tips. They are borne either singly or in pairs, on slightly hairy stems. Each is about 2.5 cm long.

■**Seeds**: Each fertilized flower carries a single, black spherical seed. The seed is hard, with a point at one end and a knob at the other.

BALINESE: *oja*
INDONESIAN: *pukul empat*
LATIN: *Mirabilis jalapa* L.; Family: *Nyctaginaceae*

Frangipani

jepun bali

There are three species of trees the Balinese call *jepun* and visitors to Asia call frangipani. One of these is described under Adenium and is not of the same genus as the true Frangipani. The wood of the *jepun bali* is prized by some of the more talented wood carvers for making free-form statues. It is also a very popular tree for planting in temples. The entrance to Pura Uluwatu on the Bukit, for example, is lined with these trees. The flowers are highly prized for offerings and decorations. *Jepun bali* is also found in Muslim cemeteries in Bali.

BALINESE: *jepun bali*
INDONESIAN: *kemboja*
LATIN: *Plumeria acuminata*; Family: *Apocynaceae*

■**Description**: A small tree, characteristically twisted and gnarled.
■**Flowers**: The flowers can be red, white, yellow, pink, or mixed, and are of two principal types. In both, the five petals are teardrop shaped, with the rounded end tapering to the base. One variety has small—12 mm—petals and is flat. The other variety has petals about twice as wide which form a tight spiral until they age and drop from the tree. Both varieties occur in various solid colors and color combinations. All varieties are strongly fragrant; none has visible flower parts.
■**Leaves**: Up to 35 cm long and 11 cm wide, though most are smaller. Both ends of the leaves are pointed.
■**Flowering**: Year-round.

Frangipani

jepun jawa

This is the most widely distributed of the frangipanis, and it can be found in almost every type of environment—along city streets, in house-compounds, and in temples and school yards. The fragrant and beautiful flowers of *jepun jawa* are an integral part of Balinese culture. They are used to decorate religious statues; women thread them in their hair, and men wear them behind an ear or stuck in a head-band.

■**Description**: Smaller, more common, and with larger flowers than *jepun bali*.
■**Flowers**: White, except for a yellow area in the center, about 7 cm across. No reproductive parts can be readily seen. The ends of the petals are almost flat, even curling under slightly.
■**Leaves**: Club-shaped, with rounded ends. They are thick and leathery, borne on short stems, and grow to 30 cm. They occur along the length of the branches, whereas the leaves of the *jepun bali* are always clustered towards the ends.
■**Flowering**: Year-round.

BALINESE: *jepun jawa*
INDONESIAN: *kemboja*
LATIN: *Plumeria obtusa*; Family: *Apocynaceae*

Garden Balsam

Garden balsam is found throughout Asia. Its most important use is for making fingernail dye. In Bali it is often grown as a cash crop, its bright red petals sold in markets for use in offerings.

BALINESE: *pacah*
INDONESIAN: *pacar, pacar air*
LATIN: *Impatiens balsamina* L.
Family: *Balsaminaceae*

■**Description**: This is a small plant with a single main stem that can grow up to 1 meter high. The stem is round, jointed, and, in some varieties, covered with stiff hairs.

■**Flowers:** Usually bright red, about 4 cm in diameter. They are irregularly shaped, having four lobed petals which overlap slightly. A fifth petal is convex with a narrow green ridge at its base that ends in a small projection. Where this petal joins the stem there are two more projections. Below this petal is a sixth, concave petal which covers the base of the flower. Where the petal joins the stem, there is a green spur about 2 cm long. Inside the flower is a bulbous pistil, 3 mm long, green and ending in a white stigma.

■**Leaves:** Stemless, serrated, long and narrow, about 13 cm long and 3.5 cm wide. The midrib is prominent while the side veins are only visible from below.

Gardenia

Gardenias are found in many gardens but are not popular in hotels because they do not bloom for long. When available, they are used in offerings. The gardenia is not to be confused with the flower called *tulud nyuh* by the Balinese. The latter is also white and grows on a small shrub very much like a gardenia. Even the leaves are similar in shape. However, the *tulud nyuh* flower is flat and has a small yellow center. It has an odor but is not quite as fragrant as the gardenia. Theoretically, *tulud nyuh* are not supposed to be used in offerings. People who have these plants, however, generally do so anyway. The Balinese name, which is probably a corruption of the Indonesian—*kaca piring*—means "glass plate."

■**Description**: This plant can grow up to 2 meters, but is usually smaller in Bali.

■**Flowers**: are about 7 cm in diameter and have 15 to 20 white, rounded petals, up to 4 cm long and 23 cm wide. The reproductive parts are not visible until the flower ages and opens wide. In the center are 5 triangular, tan

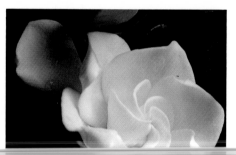

stamens. Inside the circle of stamens is a 1.5 cm long, waxy pistil with a cleft stigma. The flowers have a pleasant fragrance. The gardenia is a very fragile blossom, turning brown soon after being picked.

■**Leaves**: Glossy ovals, 8 by 3 cm, dark green. They are stemless and are paired.

BALINESE: *jempiring*
INDONESIAN: *kaca piring*
LATIN: *Gardenia florida*; Family: *Rubiaceae*

Globe Amaranth

The plant is native to the drier parts of America. In Bali, it is widely used for yard and street decoration and is commonly used in offerings and to decorate holy flags for religious ceremonies. The plants bloom for about three months, a characteristic that has inspired a sometimes heard Indonesion name, *bunga tiga bulan*—"three-month flower."

BALINESE: *ratna*
INDONESIAN: *bunga kancing*
LATIN: *Gomphrena globosa* L.
Family: *Amaranthaceae*

■**Description**: A small, shrubby annual herb with flowers in small magenta spheres that look like clover blossoms and are 1 to 3 cm across.

■**Flowers**: Each spherical flower group consists of dozens of tiny, individual flowers arranged in a tight spiral. The flowers themselves are each enclosed by two papery, magenta petals, about 1 cm long. These have white edges near the base, so that the lower part of the flower head looks whiter than the top. Within the petals is a small mass of white, fuzzy fibers ringed by 5 ribbon-like stamens. In the center of the mature flower is a white 7 mm pistil topped by a compound yellow stigma.

■**Leaves**: Fuzzy, medium green, about 6 cm long.

■**Seeds**: Small, black and produced in abundance.

■**Flowering**: During the rainy season.

Hibiscus

The Indonesian name for the hibiscus means "shoe flower." This apparently comes from the Portuguese, who used the juice of the petals to blacken shoes. There are double and single varieties. The hibiscus is to be found everywhere in Bali—in hotel gardens, along country roads, in gardens, and behind men's ears. It is commonly found in offerings and decorating tables, religious objects, and stone carvings. The roots, leaves, and flowers are sometimes used as medicine.

■**Description**: This plant has been so highly bred and selected that there are numerous varieties and it is difficult to give a general description to fit them all. Many are single flowers but there are double varieties which look like roses.

■**Flowers**: Red, white, or mixed; also, less commonly, yellow. Most varieties are characterized by a large five-petaled flower. The petals are typically pear-shaped, about 8 by 5 cm, prominently veined and somewhat wrinkled. The typical flower is about 13 cm across when fully opened. Petals overlap slightly at the base where they are frequently stained a contrasting color. Two concentric rings of triangular sepals are found beneath the petals. The pistil protrudes conspicuously from the flower, and ends in a five-branched stigma. The stamens grow as small appendages at the end of the pistil. The flower has no odor.

■**Flowering**: Year-round.

BALINESE: *pucuk*
INDONESIAN: *kembang sepatu*
LATIN: *Hibiscus rosa-sinensis* L.
Family: *Malvaceae*

Hydrangea

Many hydrangeas have been planted in the Bedugul-Candi Kuning area but few are to be found in the areas of South Bali. Nevertheless, the flowers are sold in almost every village market as they are used in offerings.

■**Description**: An herbaceous plant with clustered blossoms.
■**Flowers**: Usually a pale blue color although other varieties are sometimes seen. When the flowers first bloom, they are tinged green and only acquire their final color when they mature. Each cluster, up to 15 cm accross, has about three stems which, in turn, are divided into three or four smaller stems, each of which is compound as well. Thus, each cluster consists of 50 or more flowers. The individual flower is about 2 cm in diameter and has four more or less equally sized petals. The young flowers have yellow centers and light blue tips. The blue eventually spreads to cover the entire petal.
■**Leaves**: Medium to dark green, rounded and coarsely serrated.

BALINESE: *pasah seribu*
INDONESIAN: *bunga tiga bulan*
LATIN: *Hydrangea macrophylla*; Family: *Saxifragaceae*

Indian Laburnum

Also golden shower

The Balinese, who call the laburnum *tengguli*, do not make use of the pulp of the tree's pods although it is used in many parts of the world as a laxative. The wood is occasionally used for carvings but craftsmen say it is very hard and dulls their tools quickly. The flowers are used in offerings and the leaves are used to artificially ripen fruit. This procedure involves sealing fruit along with *tengguli* leaves in a large clay pot. A smoldering coconut-shell fire is kept burning on top of this pot for a day or two until the moist heat inside matures the fruit.

■**Description**: A tall tree distinguished by its beautiful shower of golden flowers.

■**Flowers**: In a 35 cm truss with mature blooms near the base and spherical buds at the tip. Each flower is about 4.5 cm in diameter with five yellow petals. A green pistil curls prominently from the bloom. There are 10 yellow stamens and tan anthers.

■**Leaves**: Medium to dark green leaflets in pairs along the stems; each is 12 by 7 cm and comes to a point.

■**Seeds**: In long, cylindrical pods, up to 60 cm long, green when immature but dry and brown when ripe. The flat seeds are embedded in a dark brown pulp with a faintly sweet taste.

■**Flowering**: The beginning of the rainy season, in October or November.

BALINESE: *tengguli*
INDONESIAN: *tengguli*
LATIN: *Cassia fistula*; Family: *Leguminosae*

Javanese Ixora

This is a common garden plant in Bali, and its flowers are often used in offerings. There are many in hotel gardens because they bloom all year. The Indian origin of the plant is indicated by its Indonesian and Balinese names, which make reference to Asoka, the first king of India to embrace Buddhism.

■**Description**: A medium to tall shrub that bears large, almost hemispherical clusters of flowers at the ends of its branches.

■**Flowers**: Each cluster may have has many as 60 flowers. These are usually a uniform red or orange-red although there is a so-called white variety which is actually a very pale yellow. The individual flower is small and has four spear-shaped petals, each about 1.4 cm long. These petals lie flat and are attached to a tube about 3 cm long and only 1 mm across. The buds look like match-sticks.

■**Leaves**: Oval, about 9 by 4 cm; older leaves may be quite a bit larger. They are medium to light green and somewhat glossy.

BALINESE: *soka*
INDONESIAN: *soka, kembang asoka, angsoka*
LATIN: *Ixora javanica*; Family: *Rubiaceae*

Lantana

The plant is a native of tropical America but is naturalized in Bali at elevations below 1,700 meters above sea level. The Indonesian name for the flower translates as "chicken droppings," and refers to the unpleasant odor of the entire plant. Insects and birds are attracted to the flowers and fruit. The leaves are used for treatment of ulcers, boils, and insect bites—their juice prevents bees from stinging.

■**Description**: A common woody shrub about 2 m high, sometimes taller.
■**Flowers**: Sometimes red, sometimes white, lavender, or orange. There are also mixtures of these colors. Individual flowers are small, only about 8 mm across, but grow in circular clusters about 4 to 5 cm in diameter consisting of about 30 flowers. Flowers nearer the center are more recently opened and often differ in color from the older flowers near the edges.
■**Leaves**: Grayish-green, sometimes deep green or edged deep maroon.
■**Seeds**: In berries growing in clusters.
■**Flowering**: Year-round, peaking in the rainy season.

BALINESE: *kerasi, tempuyak*
INDONESIAN: *kembang tahi ayam*
LATIN: *Lantana camara* L.; Family: *Verbenaceae*

Lotus

Also sacred lotus

The lotus is an important plant in Buddhist and Hindu symbolism. Most parts of the lotus plant are either edible or used for medicine. In Bali, lotus and water lilies are often seen growing together in hotel ponds. The Balinese use the same name to refer to both, although the two are quite different plants.

BALINESE: *tunjung*
INDONESIAN: *tunjung, teratai*
LATIN: *Nelumbium nelumbo*
Family: *Nymphaeaceae*

■**Description**: This aquatic plant produces long stalks, about 1 meter high, which bear its leaves and flowers. The stalks grow from a rhizome which lies deeply buried in the mud in pools and lakes.

■**Flowers**: Produced at the end of solitary stalks and have between 16 and 19 petals. The newly-opened flower is magenta, but when opened for a time, the tips turn purple, shading to a pale lavender—almost white—at the base. Petals are concave and tear-drop shaped, about 11 cm long and 5 cm wide, pointed at the tip. The pistil is an inverted cone, about 3 cm in diameter and 3.5 cm high, its stigma flat, with circle of dots around the edge. It looks much like a salt shaker. Dozens of stamens radiate, bristle-like, from the base of the pistil. Each is about 3 cm long, white at the bottom and yellow toward the tip. The 20-25 cm blossoms stay open only a short time. Once the petals drop, the large conical ovary is left at the end of the long stalk.

■**Leaves**: Large, round, and borne in the air.

■**Seeds**: Contained in the mature seed pod which is the hardened and enlarged conical ovary. The seed pod is brown, 6 cm high and 7 cm in diameter.

Madagascar Periwinkle

The plant is a native of tropical America and has been introduced to Bali only fairly recently.

■**Description**: This is an excellent low border plant, seldom exceeding 50 cm in height and producing a great many colorful flowers.

■**Flowers**: Red, less commonly, white and 5 cm in diameter, of a regular shape, with five symmetrical petals which are tear-drop shaped, flaring to a broad tip from a narrow base. A darker dot is visible inside the base. The stamens and pistil are so tiny as to be almost invisible.

■**Leaves**: Glossy, oval, about 6 cm long and 3 cm wide on very short stems. The midrib, being a pale green, is clearly visible.

■**Flowering**: Year-round.

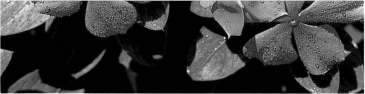

BALINESE: *tapak lima*
INDONESIAN: *kembang sari cina*
LATIN: *Vinca rosea*; Family: *Apocynaceae*

Manori

Also maduri

There is no English name for *manori*, a weed that grows vigorously on waste land and garbage dumps, and in cemeteries. A dense stand of *manori* grows near Bali's international airport on the edge of the narrow road skirting the east end of the runway. The flowers are used to prepare a material called *sadek* which is fed to fighting crickets to make them more aggressive. In some parts of Bali, the flower is used to draw cabalistic figures on the dead before cremation. The flowers of the white variety are used in offerings connected with cremations.

BALINESE: *manori, maduri*
INDONESIAN: *biduri, widuri*
LATIN: *Calotropis gigantea*; Family: *Asclepiadaceae*

■**Description**: A medium shrub that can grow to 3 m high but usually much less.
■**Flowers**: In clusters. Before they open, the buds are fluted balls of a pale lavender. These mature into lavender, or rarely, white, flowers 4 cm in diameter with five pointed petals. The flowers are of the same pale lavender as the buds with a greenish yellow center. Each petal has a small, oblong depression at the tip. The central portion of the flower is a disk, about 1.5 cm in diameter, from which arises a tiny platform bearing the stigma and stamens. Five purple ribs attach to the outside of this platform, each ending in a curl with two short horns.
■**Leaves:** Dull green, oval with pointed tips; about 7 cm long.

Mexican Lilac

This tree is native to tropical America and, although a fairly new introduction to Bali, has become well-established, especially in the drier parts. It is a useful shade tree and a source of food for cattle. Like all members of the legume family, the nitrogen-fixing bacteria on its root nodules enrich the soil.

■**Description:** Large clusters of purple to pale violet flowers along branches that are often bare of leaves distinguish this medium-sized tree. The dense clusters are reminiscent of the garden lilac but have no scent.

■**Flowers**: Pinkish lilac, about 2 cm in diameter, occurring in 10 cm long clusters. Each flower has four asymmetrical petals, one of which is larger than the rest. The base of the flower changes from green to maroon as the blooms age.

■**Leaves**: Medium green, in pairs, about 7 by 3 cm, pointed at the end.

■**Seeds***:* Contained in flat, wide pods, about 20 cm long.

■**Flowering**: Toward the end of the dry season, starting in September.

BALINESE: *gamal*
INDONESIAN: not known
LATIN: *Gliricidia sepium*; Family: *Leguminosae*

Oleander

All parts of the plant are poisonous. They contain a glucoside similar to digitalis which acts quickly, often fatally, upon the heart. This toxicity, however, does not keep the oleander from being one of the more popular decorative plants in Bali. The flowers are commonly used in offerings.

BALINESE: *kenyeri*
INDONESIAN: not known
LATIN: *Nerium indicum* Mill.; Family: *Apocynaceae*

■**Description**: There are two varieties of the common oleander, a medium to tall shrub: one has single flowers, the other, double. The flowers are red, pink, or white.

■**Flowers**: Four to 6 cm in diameter, with concave petals. The single variety has five tear-drop shaped petals. Double flowers may have up to as many as 14 petals. At the base of each petal is a 2 to 2.5 cm long part containing the stamens. The fuzzy, white pistil is 1.5 cm long. The flower has five tiny, triangular sepals. Some varieties have a faint fragrance.

■**Leaves**: Long, thin and somewhat stiff, growing up to 30 cm long and 3 cm wide. They appear in clusters of three along the twigs.

■**Seeds**: The plant forms an ellipsoidal green fruit that is 4 by 2.5 cm. Around the fruit is a ridge, perpendicular to the long axis of the fruit and extending halfway around.

Pagoda Flower

The plant is a native of tropical East Asia. Members of the genus *Clerodendron* have considerable magical significance in parts of Malaysia, but, as far as can be determined, have no such function in Bali. The plant is seen in houseyards and parks all over Bali and its flowers are commonly used in offerings.

■**Description**: The word *tumbak* in Balinese means "spear" and is applied to this medium-sized plant because of the shape of the large spike of flowers.

■**Flowers**: Reddish orange and in complex clusters about 35 cm high and 30 cm in diameter at their base. The individual flower has five orange petals about 1.5 cm in diameter which are attached to a long, thin tube containing four red stamens with brown, elliptical anthers. These, along with the long, thin, curled pistil, protrude prominently.

30 cm wide and 25 cm long, in pairs. Each leaf has five lobes and is notched at its base. The tip is a large, rounded lobe. Prominent veins lead to the tip of each lobe creating an intricate network which gives the surface of the leaf a wrinkled appearance.

BALINESE: *tumbak raja*
INDONESIAN: *senggugu*
LATIN: *Clerodendron paniculatum*
Family: *Verbenaceae*

Poinciana ✓

Also dwarf poinciana

The poinciana is common in gardens and along streets. The flowers are often used as table decorations and in offerings. One of the Balinese names for the plant, *merak*, means peacock.

BALINESE: *merak, kemerakan*
INDONESIAN: *kembang merak, kemerakan*
LATIN: *Caesalpinia pulcherrima* L.
Family: *Leguminosae*

■**Description**: A thorny shrub, often grown as a hedge, with flowers growing in spikes which may be as long as 50 cm. It will grow as tall as 4 m but is usually trimmed to about 2 m.
■**Flowers**: Have five petals, four of which are more or less the same size. These four petals are reddish-orange with wrinkled, yellow edges. In some varieties these petals are all yellow and a few may be pink with white edges. A fifth petal, located in the center, is smaller, hooded, and not striped. From this hooded petal protrude ten 5 cm long curling stamens with black anthers. The pistil is tubular, 1.5 cm long, and the same color as the edges of the petals; it looks very much like a separate flower.
■**Leaves**: Doubly compound and consist of small, medium green leaflets which may be up to 7 by 2 mm.
■**Seeds**: Flat and black, in a pod 8-12 cm long.
■**Flowering**: Year-round.

Poinsettia

Racun, the Balinese name for the poinsettia, means "poison" and most members of the *Euphorbia* family are, indeed, poisonous. The plant is a native of Mexico but has been naturalized all over the tropical and sub-tropical world, growing best at elevations below 1,200 meters above sea level.

■**Description**: The bright red "flower" of this large shrub is not really a flower at all, but rather, a cluster of bright bracts surrounding tiny, inconspicuous flowers. These bracts occur on the last several joints of the branches.

■**Flowers**: The true flower is only about 2 cm high and 1 cm across and consists of a cup-shaped green base with a red rim and yellow trim. From the center of this base grows another, smaller, inverted green cone with a red top from which protrude three tiny stigmas. Three red stamens emerge from the rim of the base.

■**Leaves**: Medium green, up to 25 cm long and 15 cm wide, with 5 points, borne singly on short stems that alternate on each side of the branches.

BALINESE: *racun, kedapa*
INDONESIAN: *kastuba*
LATIN: *Euphorbia pulcherrima* Willd.; Family: *Euphorbiaceae*

Purple Orchid Tree

Also purple bauhinia

This tree is a fairly recent introduction to Bali. The Indonesian Department of Forestry has nurseries where the seedlings are grown; these are provided to the various municipal districts for planting along the roads. The purple orchid tree is to be seen lining the streets in Denpasar, Sanur, and Kuta, among many other places. The Indonesian and Balinese names for the tree, *Kupu-kupu*, means "butterfly" and is applied to the purple orchid tree because the leaves look like this insect.

BALINESE: *sabita*, *kupu-kupu*
INDONESIAN: *daun kupu-kupu*
LATIN: *Bauhinia purpurea*; Family: *Fabaceae*

■**Description:** This medium-sized tree is distinguished by its twin-lobed leaves.

■**Flowers**: Purple to pale violet or pink, 8 to 10 cm in diameter, with five, long, thin, petals, one slightly shorter than the rest, located asymmetrically. The petals have a slightly wrinkled appearance. Three long, purple stamens curl out prominently together with the shorter, light green pistil.

■**Leaves**: Light green, leathery, 15 cm wide and 14 cm long, the leaves look like two joined ellipses with a V-shaped indentation at the joint.

■**Seeds**: The tree produces long, flat beans with a curled, pointed tip. The pods are about 20 cm long.

■**Flowering**: During the dry season, from July until around October.

Rose of India

Also crepe flower

The dense foliage of this tree makes it ideal for shade. Many have been planted along the streets of Denpasar and Renon as well as along the By-Pass Highway.

■**Description**: A medium-sized tree with dense foliage, and purple to pale violet or pink flowers clustered closely in a spike.

■**Flowers**: about 7 cm in diameter with six petals that look somewhat ragged because of their wavy edges and wrinkled surfaces. Each petal consists of a spade-shaped section attached to a thin stem. The center is a mass of thin, white stamens ending in yellow anthers. There is one white pistil, about 2 cm long.

■**Leaves**: Medium green with slightly wavy, but not serrated, edges. Each is almost perfectly oval and terminates in a short, point-ed tip. They are about 20 cm long, 10 cm wide, and paired along the twigs.

■**Seeds**: Small and winged, contained in a brown, hard, nut-like sphere with a cap of six dried sepals.

■**Flowering**: Occurs toward the end of the dry season, usually around the beginning of September.

BALINESE: t*angi*
INDONESIAN: b*ungur*
LATIN: *Lagerstroemia speciosa* (L.) Pers.
Family: *Lythraceae*

Sandat

The very fragrant flowers of the *sandat*—no common English name exists—are favored by the Balinese for offerings; they are picked very early in the morning and can be found in every market in Bali. The *sandat* is also used to perfume hair and clothing. An essential oil is extracted from the flower to scent soaps, cosmetics and perfume. This oil is sometimes given a yellow color by frying the flowers in turmeric. The leaves are used as a medicine for malaria and the bark of the tree provides material for twine.

BALINESE: *sandat*
INDONESIAN: *kenanga*
LATIN: *Cananga odorata* Baill.
Family: *Annonaceae*

■**Description:** The inconspicuous, green flowers are often difficult to see because they occur high in this tall tree.
■**Flowers:** Long, narrow, and limp, light green in color, changing to a pale lemon yellow when fully open. There are six somewhat wrinkled petals, each about 5 to 8 cm long and 1 to 1.5 cm wide at the widest point. The center of the flower is complex, consisting of tiny stamens and a compound stigma.
■**Leaves:** Medium green, almost perfectly spear-shaped, occuring alternately. They range in size from 20 by 9 cm to 30 by 13 cm. Veining makes the surface seem wrinkled.
■**Seeds:** About a dozen 2 by 1.5 cm fruits on a spike.
■**Flowering:** Year-round.

Senna

This plant is a native of India. The Balinese name, *koning*, means "yellow." In some parts of Indonesia the leaves are eaten and medicinal properties are attributed to both roots and leaves. The flowers are commonly used in offerings.

■**Description**: A shrub which normally grows to about 2-3 meters.
■**Flowers**: Yellow and between 6 and 7 cm in diameter, with five petals in the shape of tear-drops. Three of them are larger than the other two, being about 3 cm long and 2 cm wide at the widest point. Of the two other petals, one is round and convex, the other is a modified sheath for the reproductive organs. In the center are seven thick, yellow, crescent-shaped stamens, each 1 cm long, and a 2.5 cm long curved, green pistil. The flowers hang down like clusters of bells, most of them being rather limp, with petals hanging straight down.
■**Leaves**: Compound, consisting of stemless, medium green leaflets that are somewhat curved, roughly 12 cm long and 5 cm wide.

BALINESE: *koning, kuning*
INDONESIAN: not known
LATIN: *Cassia surattensis*; Family: *Fabaceae*

Thunbergia ✓

The Balinese name for thunbergia is simply the plural of the word blue—*pelung-pelung*. The plant commonly grows along the road in hedges and the Balinese regularly use thunbergia flowers in offerings. Rare is the *canang*, the small coconut leaf offerings that are everywhere on the island, that does not contain a bright, blue-violet *pelung-pelung* blossom.

BALINESE: *pelung-pelung*
INDONESIAN: not known
LATIN: *Thunbergia natalensis*; Family: *Acanthaceae*

■**Description**: Thunbergia will grow unsupported as a low shrub, but, if given support, will grow into a woody vine, several meters high.

■**Flowers**: The five petals are almost completely fused into a flaring trumpet, separated only at their ends. The flower is about 4.5 cm in diameter and about 6 cm long. Each petal is notched at the center, at the lip of the flower. The inner portion of the funnel is a bright yellow. The outside is brilliant purple around the lip, fading to white at the base. Deep inside the funnel are four stamens with tufted tips and one white pistil about 2.5 cm long.

■**Leaves**: Spear-shaped leaflets, about 4.5 cm long and 2 cm wide occur in pairs along the stem at intervals of 3-4 cm. Leaf veins are not prominent.

Tree Hibiscus

There is considerable confusion over the Balinese nomenclature of this tree. There is, in fact, only one type of tree hibiscus, or *waru*. However, since the wood of the *waru* varies with the particular environment in which it has grown, being spongy or hard, dark or light, the Balinese use different names for members of the same species: *waru taluh, waru tutup, waru pulet,* etc. Some call it hibiscus; some confuse it with *waru lot,* which is a different tree altogether. To make matters worse, many people give the name hibiscus to *waru lot, Thespesia populnea* L., which, though of the same botanical family, is not the same genus as either *waru* or hibiscus.

■**Description**: The tree may reach a height of 15 meters, but is usually lopped off.

■**Flowers**: Bright yellow trumpets. They look something like the familiar hibiscus, but are smaller, lack protuding pistils, and remain closed until almost ready to drop. They occur in clusters of five or more at the ends of branches. As the flower ages, it deepens to a dark maroon. The flower eventually opens fully and drops, whirling to the ground like a pinwheel.

■**Leaves**: Almost round except for a short, stubby tip, 16 cm in diameter.

■**Seeds**: Flat, 3 cm sphere.

■**Flowering**: Irregular, but usually at start of rainy season.

BALINESE: *waru*
INDONESIAN: *waru*
LATIN: *Hibiscus tiliaceus* L.; Family, *Malvaceae*

Virgin Tree

Also aurorae, Buddha's lamp

This plant is a native of the Philippines but has been natural-ized in Bali and can be found decorating streets and gardens. The Balinese and Indonesian names mean "beautiful island." Although the flowers are odorless, they are used in offerings.

BALINESE: *nusa indah*
INDONESIAN: *nusa indah*
LATIN: *Mussaenda philippica*
Family: *Rubiaceae*

■**Description**: A popular ornamental shrub or small tree. The colored parts of this plant are bracts, rather than petals, and can be pink, white, or very rarely, red.

■**Flowers**: The actual flower is a small five-pointed star, 1.7 cm in diameter. Each pet-al has a sharp ridge running radially down its center. The flower is usually a bright orange or yellow or, in the case of the variety with bright red bracts, white. It is positioned on a thin, green tube, about 2.5 cm long and 3 mm in diameter. Five bracts surround each flower. Since the flowers are clus-tered together at the ends of the branches, the effect is of a large mass of color. The mature bracts are about 4 by 7 cm.

■**Leaves**: Medium green, oval, pointed at each end, about 13 cm long and 6 cm wide. Veining makes the surface of the appear wrinkled. They are borne on short stems in pairs.

Water Convolvulus

The water convolvulus is common in Southeast Asian and Chinese cooking. The Chinese call it *kong xin cai*, or "empty heart vegetable," on account of its distinctive hollow stems. The Balinese distinquish two types of what they call *kangkung*: *kangkung air* (an aquatic variety) and *kangkung darat* (the "dry" variety). *Kangkung* is used mainly as a vegetable.

■**Description**: A low spreading vine.

■**Flowers**: Large, trumpet- shaped, and about 5 cm in diameter with bright purple or magenta centers. The petals are fused together and are creased down the middle with a small notch at their tips. Deep within the flower's cylindrical cup are five short, thin stamens, each about 1 cm long, and a slightly longer pistil with a relatively large white stigma.

■**Leaves**: Heart-shaped and elongated, up to 11 cm long and 8 cm wide, deeply notched at the base and tapering to a long, thin point.

■**Flowering**: Year-round.

BALINESE: *kangkung*
INDONESIAN: *kangkung*
LATIN: *Ipomoea aquatica*; Family: *Convolvulaceae*

Water Lily

Like the lotus, water lilies are important flowers in offerings and are grown in Bali for that purpose. Almost all parts of the plant are edible or used for medicines, though not in Bali. Water lilies are planted in large pots which are placed at the bottom of shallow pools. In the wild, the rhizome lies deeply buried in the mud at the bottom of stillwater ponds and pools.

BALINESE: *tunjung*
INDONESIAN: *padma, teratai*
LATIN: *Nymphaea lotus*
Family: *Nymphaeaceae*

■**Description**: An aquatic plant with large, floating leaves. The flowers either float or protrude slightly above the water.
■**Flowers**: About 9 by 2.5 cm, with 25 petals. In many cases, the petals are convex with a small black stain at the tip. Inside the flower is a circle of long, thin, flat stamens which are a bright yellow or red in the mature flower. Each is 4.5 cm long with a rounded anther. Within this circle is another circular group of shorter stamens, each stained with a purple stripe. In the case of the white lily, they are sometimes all yellow. Yet another circle of stamens is found in the very center.
■**Leaves**: Dark green to dark red, about 24 by 22 cm with a deep slit where they are attached to their dark red stems. The edges of the leaves are wrinkled.
■**Flowering**: Year-round.

Widelia

In Balinese, this plant is called *padang lumut-lumut. Padang* means"grass" or "plant," and *lumut* means "moss." When the plant is wet, it becomes as slippery as moss. It is often used as a border for walks and lawns. In the villages, it is used widely as cattle food. The flowers are used for table decorations.

■**Description**: There are quite a few varieties of this plant. Some are vines.

■**Flowers**: Yellow composites, 2 to 2.5 cm in diameter and bearing 9 to 11 petals each 1 cm long and 4 mm wide. The tips terminate in two notches. In the center of the flower is a group of about 25 tiny, prismatic parts which terminate in paired yellow stamens. Below the stamens a black tube connects to the ovary.

■**Leaves**: Glossy, with a central lobe and curved edges. They often have two sharp projections on the side and their bases envelop the stem of the vine. They are typically 5-6 cm long and 3.5-4 cm wide.

BALINESE: *padang lumut-lumut*
INDONESIAN: *serunai rambat*
LATIN: *Widelia trilobata*; Family: *Compositae*

Yellow Bells

Also yellow trumpet flower

Yellow bells are commonly found along the roads and in house-yards. The plant is a native of tropical America. In Bali it is used purely as an ornamental.

■**Description**: A bushy shrub or small tree bearing clusters of yellow flowers at the ends of its branches.

■**Flowers**: Trumpet-shaped, about 3 cm in diameter and 4 cm long, on very short, green stems. Each flower has five semi-circular, 1 cm long petals with flattened tips which are fused together at the base to form a long, tapering funnel. Inside the funnel, at the top, are two raised ribs. The lines are not visible on the outside of the flower. The yellowish-brown, T-shaped anthers of two stamens are just visible inside the flower. They are borne at the ends of two long, pale green filaments. Deeper in the cup are two similar, shorter stamens and one pale pistil with a bulbous ovary.

■**Leaves**: Stemless, 8.5 by 2.5 cm, coarsely-serrated leaflets.

■**Seeds**: Flat and oval, about 6 by 3 mm. They are borne in skinny, flat pods, about 18 cm long, 7 mm wide, and 3 mm thick.

BALINESE: *kenyeri*
INDONESIAN: not known
LATIN: *Stenolobium stans*; Family: *Bignoniaceae*

Index by Latin name

Hydrangea macrophylla	hydrangea	34
Impatiens balsamina L.	garden balsam	30
Ipomoea aquatica	water convolvulus	53
Ixora javanica	Javanese ixora	36
Lagerstroemia speciosa (L) Pers.	rose of India	47
Lantana camara L.	lantana	37
Malvafiscus sp.	firecracker hibiscus	25
Michelia champaca L.	champak	15
Mirabilis jalapa L.	four o'clock	27
Musa sp.	banana	10
Mussaenda philippica	virgin tree	52
Nelumbium nelumbo	lotus	38
Nerium indicum Mill.	oleander	42
Nymphaea lotus	water lily	54
Plumeria acuminata	frangipani	28
Plumeria obtusa	frangipani	29
Spathodea campanulata	African tulip tree	8
Stenolobium stans	yellow bells	56
Thunbergia natalensis	thunbergia	50
Vinca rosea	Madagascar periwinkle	39
Widelia trilobata	widelia	55

Index by Balinese name

kupu-kupu	purple orchid tree	46
maduri	(none)	40
manori	(none)	40
merak	flamboyant	26
merak	poinciana	44
nusa indah	virgin tree	52
nyuh	coconut	19
oja	four o'clock	27
pacah	garden balsam	30
pandang lumut-lumut	widelia	55
pasah seribu	hydrangea	34
pelung-pelung	thunbergia	50
pucuk	hibiscus	33
pucuk geringsing	coral hibiscus	21
pucuk tabia-tabia	firecracker hibiscus	25
racun	poinsettia	45
ratna	globe amaranth	32
sabita	purple orchid tree	46
sandat	(none)	48
semprong	datura	23
soga	canna	13
soka	Javanese ixora	36
sungsang	climbing lily	17
sungsiang	climbing lily	17
tapak lima	Madagascar periwinkle	39
tangi	rose of India	47
tempuyak	lantana	37
tengguli	Indian laburnum	35
tumbak raja	pagoda flower	43
tunjung	lotus	38
tunjung	water lily	54
waru	tree hibiscus	51